I0766253

USA: HERE'S HOW TRUMP WINS IN 2020.

Washington, D.C., United States of America.

FIRST EDITION, 2019.

USA

HERE'S HOW TRUMP WINS IN 2020

Thums • Sevilla

This book is dedicated to the only person we
know can win in 2020.

Thums & Sevilla

A NOTE FROM THE AUTHORS

This book is intended for patriots to express their first amendment right in a collaborative effort with the authors in the hopes of inspiring other Americans. In the following pages, you are asked to contribute so that you may help choose the next President of the United States.

<u>Here's how:</u> By sharing your stories, raising your voice, quoting your favorite speeches, and identifying media bias, you will help make this campaign even greater.

Please upload your work, and comments using the hashtag #hereshow and let's show them how Trump will win in 2020!

Thums • Sevilla

USA: Here's How Trump Wins in 2020

9

Thums • Sevilla

USA: Here's How Trump Wins in 2020

USA: Here's How Trump Wins in 2020

USA: Here's How Trump Wins in 2020

USA: Here's How Trump Wins in 2020

USA: Here's How Trump Wins in 2020

USA: Here's How Trump Wins in 2020

USA: Here's How Trump Wins in 2020

USA: Here's How Trump Wins in 2020

USA: Here's How Trump Wins in 2020

USA: Here's How Trump Wins in 2020

Thums • Sevilla

USA: Here's How Trump Wins in 2020

USA: Here's How Trump Wins in 2020

USA: Here's How Trump Wins in 2020

USA: Here's How Trump Wins in 2020

Thums • Sevilla

USA: Here's How Trump Wins in 2020

USA: Here's How Trump Wins in 2020

USA: Here's How Trump Wins in 2020

USA: Here's How Trump Wins in 2020

USA: Here's How Trump Wins in 2020

USA: Here's How Trump Wins in 2020

USA: Here's How Trump Wins in 2020

USA: Here's How Trump Wins in 2020

Thums • Sevilla

USA: Here's How Trump Wins in 2020

USA: Here's How Trump Wins in 2020

USA: Here's How Trump Wins in 2020

USA: Here's How Trump Wins in 2020

Thums • Sevilla

USA: Here's How Trump Wins in 2020

51

53

54

57

USA: Here's How Trump Wins in 2020

61

USA: Here's How Trump Wins in 2020

USA: Here's How Trump Wins in 2020

USA: Here's How Trump Wins in 2020

USA: Here's How Trump Wins in 2020

USA: Here's How Trump Wins in 2020

75

Thums • Sevilla

USA: Here's How Trump Wins in 2020

Thums • Sevilla

USA: Here's How Trump Wins in 2020

Thums • Sevilla

USA: Here's How Trump Wins in 2020

Thums • Sevilla

USA: Here's How Trump Wins in 2020

USA: Here's How Trump Wins in 2020

USA: Here's How Trump Wins in 2020

USA: Here's How Trump Wins in 2020

USA: Here's How Trump Wins in 2020

USA: Here's How Trump Wins in 2020

Thums • Sevilla

USA: Here's How Trump Wins in 2020

USA: Here's How Trump Wins in 2020

USA: Here's How Trump Wins in 2020

USA: Here's How Trump Wins in 2020

USA: Here's How Trump Wins in 2020

USA: Here's How Trump Wins in 2020

USA: Here's How Trump Wins in 2020

Thums • Sevilla

USA: Here's How Trump Wins in 2020

USA: Here's How Trump Wins in 2020

USA: Here's How Trump Wins in 2020

USA: Here's How Trump Wins in 2020

Thums • Sevilla

USA: Here's How Trump Wins in 2020

USA: Here's How Trump Wins in 2020

USA: Here's How Trump Wins in 2020

USA: Here's How Trump Wins in 2020

USA: Here's How Trump Wins in 2020

USA: Here's How Trump Wins in 2020

Thums • Sevilla

USA: Here's How Trump Wins in 2020

Thums • Sevilla

USA: Here's How Trump Wins in 2020

USA: Here's How Trump Wins in 2020

USA: Here's How Trump Wins in 2020

USA: Here's How Trump Wins in 2020

USA: Here's How Trump Wins in 2020

149

USA: Here's How Trump Wins in 2020

USA: Here's How Trump Wins in 2020

USA: Here's How Trump Wins in 2020

USA: Here's How Trump Wins in 2020

USA: Here's How Trump Wins in 2020

USA: Here's How Trump Wins in 2020

USA: Here's How Trump Wins in 2020

USA: Here's How Trump Wins in 2020

USA: Here's How Trump Wins in 2020

USA: Here's How Trump Wins in 2020

www.ingramcontent.com/pod-product-compliance
Lightning Source LLC
Chambersburg PA
CBHW031120250726

48655CB00004B/1771